CANTICLES

A Collection of Poems

LEILA DUTT SEN

INDIA • SINGAPORE • MALAYSIA

Canticles
A Collection of Poems

Published by Notion Press, Chennai, India
First edition 2016
Second edition 2023

www.leilasen.com

Library of Congress Cataloguing-in-Publication Data is on file

ISBN 978-93-5206-816-6

To Ronjon,

for whom, through our years apart and together,
many of these poems were written

CONTENTS

A Book of Verses underneath the Bough,
A Jug of Wine, a Loaf of Bread – and Thou
Beside me singing in the Wilderness…

– Omar Khayyam

PRELUDE

If empty hours you would dispel,
Sweet Muse for you here peals her bell;
Bright Fancy dreams, and cards her spell;
These minstrels' ballads I but tell.

Charmed lay and lore, from far and near,
In canticles are gathered here
To spin a silken web, so sheer,
Upon your eye and 'round your ear.

So, rest a while now, shut your eye.
Pray, choose your fav'rite lullaby.
On glitt'ring word and dulcet sigh,
Soar! Like yon dancing dragonfly!

MORNING SONG

Far in the kindled, erubescent east
The dark spirit of night has just deceased;
And, like a vast hued and painted scroll,
Slowly the dew-crumpled clouds unroll.
Now, over a pearl'd rim the tousled dawn
Bursts into the opal bubble of morn!
Drowsy morn! Still wrapped in a swaddling mist
Of soft slumber, dreams her moist face is kissed
By the golden sun on his fiery steed
As he rides o'er heaven and earthly mead.
Plump, pillaging bees tipple from flowers
Gold nectar-wine stilled of May-dew showers.
The sweet paean of a matin breeze is heard,
Dancing to the warble of the bulbul bird.
Over yonder wood and verdurous glen
Sylvan sunlight scribbles with her gold pen.
She's risen, but now, from a waking dream,
Caught tangled in the ripples of a silver stream.
Bright eyed day, begilded with golden blush,
Embraces the world in a radiant crush.
Look! The sky with pinions of light is torn
And, behold, how a whole new day is born!

EVENSONG

The portals of dusk are gently closing
Upon the earth which is softly dozing.
Pale evening lies stilled in the twilight hush
As a dove's love song turns her cheeks to blush.
Outside my window an astonished leaf
Stutters and falls with a soft sigh of grief.
The plaintive lament from a cowherd's flute
Floats out of a ripe grove of mango fruit.
It startles a maiden, beauteous fair,
Of burnt-ivory skin and midnight-black hair.
Naughty nymph! She has pilfered bounties sweet;
Look, the juice still sticks to her hands and feet.
Beware! One fruit may breed the canker deep
Of the grub in a curlicue of sleep.
Great cloud vaults fill with a storm-laden breeze
That laughs and sings to the tremulous trees;
Stories and songs of the great monsoon rain,
Till the woods resound to its wild refrain.
Gold bubbles of rainshine now bounce and break
On the pristine face of yon dreaming lake,
Till its rain-spangled waters leap and prance
With crystal-edged shadows in buoyant dance.
Horses of thunder flash, galloping fast,
Swift hooves streak lightening as they fly past
With passion swept rain-winds that perfume the earth,

Annointing her loins with the sweet scent of birth.
Sundown, at last, rests his languorous feet,
Arduous journey done, his task complete.
He waits for bejewelled lady-night now,
With sweet, sleep-silvered lips to kiss his brow.
'Way, down by the sea, the sad seagull's cry
Faints through the fast fading cerulean sky.
A moon-polished mist drenched with jasmine flowers
Hangs shimmering veils 'round the gloaming hours.
The tendrils of night have quietly curled
Around the edge of a sleep-darkened world.
See the moon! A pale, wanton harem slave
In abandoned dance on a star cobbled wave.
She drowns in the arms of the ardent sea,
Like a lovelorn maid lost in ecstasy!

REPOSE AND RESURRECTION

The cowled and hooded face of day
Is glimpsed as evening slips away
To glide between the silken folds
Of night. The peeping moon beholds
Her shed her sable camisole
And shut her luminous eyes of kohl.
His gilded fingers fondly brush
Her lang'rous limbs with burnished blush;
Then, drape her in a gauzy sheet
Of muslin mists, from head to feet.
Her slumber, sweet a thousandfold
With dreams, from whence, in cloth of gold
She'll rise anon in burst of light,
With glitt'ring crown and sceptre bright,
To lift the dazzling veil of dawn
And bare the dew-drenched face of morn.
Blithe alabaster sprite of day,
Come, dance, make merry while you may,
Till gloaming's footfalls sound once more
As she knocks softly at dusk's door.

THE GLOAMING

Old Mother Gloaming embroiders the sky…
A jeweled tapestry of rainbow dye,
Fringed with plush tassels of dark-velvet night
And needle-point stitches of silver light;
With clouds all a-tumble, like silken bales
Of billowing black and navy-blue sails.
Now, a magical hush lies over the world…
See! A large, amber harvest-moon is hurl'd
Like a scuttling ghost ship that swells and dips
Through ebony seas kissed by moonbeam lips.

THE HOUR OF COWDUST
'GO-DHOOLI BELA'

A gaunt Indian village nestles
at the knee of yonder hill;
Faint goatbells tinkle softly,
the summer's eve stands very still.
From yonder gently resting fields
see the toilworn farmhands plod,
Bowed backs still wet with noonday sweat,
dusty, footsore and unshod.
The meagre evening meal cooks slow
on smoky dung-cake fires;
The cowherd and his lowing calves
pass that morning's funeral pyres.
The golden haze of hoof-dust hangs
in the parched and baking air,
Mother Night has yet to throw her veils
of dew with tender care.
Her benison of evening fills the west
with a hallowed flame
From the crimson lamp of twilight
which she burns in *Vishnu's** name.
Crouched, cowpat huts with thatched roofs
bend their patient, soundless gaze
Across pondering fields of whisper-filled
paddy-rice and maize.

Here, in the cool of the Champa tree,
by the bank of a murm'ring stream,
'Neath boughs of swaying milk-blossom,
I float away in a perfumed dream.
'Tis the time of day for worship,
heavy incense rises high,
The age-old chant of the Brahmin priest
is slowly wafting by.
The mellow toll of temple bells
fills the dusk with silver song.
The plaintive call of the sacred conch
beckons a faithful throng.
Mistress Moon is risen from her sleep
and sails the night-lake sky,
Hush! Somewhere midst the mango flowers
I hear a *koel*** cry.
My village kinfolk are abed now,
a hard day's rest they reap.
Come, my trusty well-worn sandals,
let us homeward wend to sleep.

Vishnu: Hindu god of Preservation, part of the holy Hindu trinity.
***koel* or *kokil:* bird of the cuckoo family.

TO BENGAL

The rice fields are calling to me in waves of green song. The early morning is breaking forth with blessings in the eastern sky. Like the yolk of a carelessly broken egg, the sun has dripped gold upon waking groves of gentle bamboo. Standing tall and stalwart, young coconut palms steal a bold, mirrored kiss from the reticent waters of the village pond where fish leap among dancing *shapla** and lotus blossom, like silver-belled chorus girls fracturing their dew-jewelled dreams. Deep and dense, the sultry *kochuripana*** spreads her tangled green tresses; a lush, floating carpet, the sapphire blossoms like tears of longing she weeps in her reach for the *kathchampa's**** alluring fragrance that beckons from the water's edge. Over yonder, a teasing breeze, like some secret courtesan, trails inviting fingers through tender rice fields that tremble with desire at her siren song. It fills the air, whisper-sweet, enticing the brash laugh of a *kokil***** who darts out of hiding; his call, clarion clear through the glistening morning dew, bursts in the sunlight with the sweetness of a ripened fruit. As though rooted in eternity, the ancient banyan tree watches…waits…and smiles in tranquil reflection. My village shakes the dust of yesterday from its thatched roof as it washes itself in the cool promise of today.

Ah! Would I were there that I might slake this thirst and partake of the simple feast of life!

*water lily

**water hyacinth

***plumeria, frangipani, temple flower

****bird of the cuckoo family

FOUR MAIDS FAIR

Dance light, oh lovely lass of Spring,
Your gown of flowers billowing!
With sun-washed, dew-kissed feet you skip
And perfumed mouth sweet nectar sip.

Awake! Fair, fulsome Summer's wench,
Caught fast asleep on garden bench.
All supped on berries, stained with wine
And garlanded with fruit of vine.

Fly, brilliant, burnished Autumn maid
Of coppered skin and auburn braid.
You hide and seek in leaf-strewn dell
And, laughing, sound late Summer's knell.

Hail! Regal, radiant Winter's Queen
With snowy crown and glitt'ring mien.
Where north wind blows and hoar frost nips,
There have you touched your icy lips.

Each lays her head on changing mead,
Hillock, woodland, by rush and reed;
Sired each twelvemonth, sisters four,
Come, strew your bounties at my door!

SOUL DANCE
THE SUBMISSION:

I am windsong, I am light,
Hear my song of pure delight.
Set me free and see me soar,
Like a bugle I will pour
Joyful music, clear and true,
And bathe myself in golden hue.
Watch me flutter, watch me fly;
See me drown in the trembling sky.
Release my soul, unbind this snare!
But, if my fragile dreams you'll share,
Stand by me, love, and take your place;
Come, join this bright and painful race.
We will change from storm to breeze,
Pass from turbulence to peace;
Fill thirsting spirit and hung'ring mind,
And see through eyes no longer blind!

ROMANCE OR REALITY
THE RESPONSE:

"I am windsong, I am light,
Hear my song of pure delight."

Delightful, singer, though it be,
It is of an erstwhile century.

"But, listen…how this voice can soar!
Like a bugle I will pour
Joyful music, clear and true,
To bathe this world in golden hue."

This world is stoically here and now.
Pragmatic trend must disavow
Those archaic songs of yesteryear,
Sweet though they fall upon the ear.

"Their sweetness if you comprehend,
Then, hear me sing to you, my friend.
Watch me flutter, watch me fly,
See me drown in the trembling sky!"

Alas! It seems your time is past.
'Realism' is your iconoclast;
Misplaced, miscast, untimely star,
Anachronism that you are!

BLINDFOLDS

This crazy world of troubled times
Has learnt but naught from all the crimes
Perpetrated throughout the years.
Ripped and torn, and quite parched of tears,
Still to its headlong course it keeps,
From war to war it madly leaps.
Seems man's destructive force must rend,
And bring about a fitting end.
But Nature, with much tender care,
Fills each sad rift and mends each tear.
Gravely she saves each piece, to then,
Render us whole and healed again.
And the world goes on, unaware
Of the sorrow we make her bear.

DESTINY

Freedom beats its useless wings and has nowhere to go,
Eyes blinded by the endless glare of empty days on show.
Joy which often seems so near, yet slips just out of reach,
The lessons Man was meant to learn,
the Fates are wont to teach.
Poor, desperate, lunging mortal mind, its fibre rent by toil,
Cold Destiny's unheeding hand will very often foil.
The frailty of the human heart that begs and pleads parole,
Blindfolded Fates, those Sisters Three*,
must needs extract their toll.
A victim of his need to share
his life and circumstance...
But stone-deaf Luck turns her face
with ne'er a cursory glance.
The woeful, yearning last resort
as Man then hocks his soul,
In futile hope of paying the price
to render him heart-whole!

*The Fates: three sister goddesses, sometimes known as the Moirai,
or Parcae

NO ROSE GARDEN

It's up at six and work at eight
And, Lord forbid, you should be late!
The morning's such a battleground,
Fraught with disaster. Look around:

The bathroom's messed, the bed's unmade…
No time for them – with stocks to trade,
Boardroom meetings, a bus to catch –
Just grab your bag and turn that latch.

Those dratted keys! Where could they be?
Must skip breakfast for, as you see,
The juice is spilt, the coffee's cold,
The toast is burnt and one day old!

'Wait! It's your turn to feed the cat.'
'I'm late already, you do that.'
'But, I must get to work as well.
I'm just as rushed. Or can't you tell?'

'Hey, I know! But I can't talk now.'
(Tension tightens your furrowed brow.)
'Could you pick up the laundry, then?'
'Might not be home till after ten.'

This selfish grouch who shares your house,
You chose this 'prince' to call your spouse?
Your live-in lover? This gruff bear?
Oh, head take heed and heart beware!

At work you have no time to breathe,
Your nerves are frayed and tempers seethe –
Clients to soothe, deadlines to meet –
By five you're quite dead on your feet.

At home at last! You've paid your dues!
Shrug off your coat, kick off your shoes…
What!! The TV's turned to news at eight,
He's sprawled on the couch to vegetate?!!

'Oh no you don't! Pick up your mess.
I'm just fed-up, I must confess.
You promised you would share the chores,
Help cook and clean and fetch our stores.

Those were the terms, we both agreed.
I'm not your servant, no indeed!
And pouting there with that childish frown
Won't help clean up or calm me down.

So – you cook dinner, I'll wash the pots.'
'Oh no! Why should you call the shots?
I'll wash the pots; you fix the meal.
To me that sounds the fairer deal.'

'A deal is it! You talk of fair?
I don't know how you even dare!
You've turned into a selfish heel
And don't consider how I feel.

You've broken every promise made.
For trusting you, I've dearly paid.
What a mistake! Well, now, I'm through.
I've finally had enough of you!'

(Sweet words once vowed in throes of bliss,
Then sealed with love's eternal kiss,
When hurled like angry sticks and stones
Will bruise frail hearts, if break no bones!) *

Packed suitcase dragged across the floor;
Angry footsteps, a slammed front door.
Sudden silence. You stand and glare…
Oh, good riddance! Why should you care!

It wasn't your fault, that's for sure.
There's just so much one can endure.
And being single is not so bad.
All things considered, you're…sort of…glad.

Days seem empty and nights seem long;
Rather lonely when you don't belong.
You should be happy, and relieved;
Instead you're feeling…somewhat peeved.

Till death do us part? What a joke
Foisted on unsuspecting folk!
In truth, for better or for worse
Seems much to hinge on heft of purse!

Days are long and nights are empty;
You're lying awake at three-twenty.
Snuggling up to the purring cat,
You reconsider that final spat.

You shared some great times, did you not?
If less than perfect at times…so what?
Shared joys are doubled, sorrows halved –
An axiom out of wisdom carved.

But wisdom may prove a painful thing
Begat in place of your wedding ring!
What use are TV, couch or house
Bereft of lover or of spouse?

Maybe a casual phone 'hello' –
You bear no grudge. You'd like to know
If all is well. And what is new.
Is there another…uh…in place of you?

Perhaps just meeting might be fun.
So much you'd planned was left undone.
Shared hopes too precious to forego,
And values, hard won, you now know!

Sincerity, trust, requited love,
A friend whom you treasured above
All others you've since come across.
(You've learnt to glean the gold from dross!)

Should you, per chance, both feel the same,
You might accept…life was to blame.
Love's ups and downs, no easy street;
Maneuvering through proved no mean feat!

Yet…better by far for two than one
To face those days of storm and sun.
So…should you agree…if apropos…
Would you, old friend, please let me know?

* Children's nursery rhyme: 'Sticks and stones may hurt my bones, but words will never harm me'

THE DOUBLE-EDGED ARABESQUE

An early morning sky bereft of tears,
Its clouds etched with pain and aged with years.
A rainsoaked evening on hushed wings of light,
The silver patter of the feet of night.
Their ardent tryst that blooms at full-blown noon,
The steep death glissade which comes all too soon.

White sea horses ride the crest of a wave;
Masqued darkness dances in a coral cave.
The nascent blush of daylight in the east,
Its frenzied abandon at a gloaming feast.
The shadowy etchings of joy and pain,
Like a sunlit tear through the golden rain.

June's gilt calligraphy across a cloud,
Hints not of winter in its darkling shroud;
Full-bodied May threads garlands of flowers
Touched by brilliant fingered April showers.
Echoes of laughter sigh on Autumn's breath:
Eternal arabesque of Life and Death.

TAKE MY HAND

Take my hand and come with me, and we will walk through the garden of life, where soft grasses will cushion our footfalls and gentle breezes will cool our brow; where trees shall yield unto us their fruit, and leaves whisper unto us their secrets. And, with the first kiss of dusk upon the evening, a songbird shall sing to us of slumber, a gossamer web of melody woven about the night. You are entranced, beloved; your senses are lulled, your mind is drugged with the opiate of ease. No sorrow can come nigh you, and I am, perhaps, a forgotten shadow at your side.

But what matters it! For, one day, perchance you come upon the thorn of a rose, I shall be there to succour you and draw the pain from your wound, so we may continue along the pathway of life, side by side, hand in hand. And, what matters it if round yonder bend you stumble upon a hidden pebble. What, have you so little faith that you cry out in fear! Am I not beside you to bear your weight upon my shoulders? For, there is such a joy in sharing that I cannot speak of it. But, at our journey's end, you will look into my eyes and you will see a silent blessing, for I will give thanks that we did share this life together. I could not want for more.

Give me your answer then, beloved – come, will you walk with me? Will you be my life?

A DISCOVERED THOUGHT

A lissom thought from quiescence born
In the pearl-grey lustre of early dawn.
First, it swirls around my quivering mind
Like the morning mist that creeps up behind
The furled edge of night, on the fringe of day.
Like a mellow breeze in the mid of May,
It whispers and comforts my weary brain,
Its touch turning my thoughts from mad to sane.
And, just as the rose-tinted morning dew
Glints molten when sunlight transforms its hue
From cool, brilliant crystal to flashing flame…
So, my soul is afire as it lays claim
To that small share of heaven we have found
In this corner on earth turned hallowed ground
By a love that is flowing 'twixt you and me,
Boundless and deep as the infinite sea.
It transforms my world to a radiant place,
Lit by the promise I see in your face.
And I pray that my part in the creative plan
Is to stand by your side for as long as I can.

DÉJÀ VU

The jewel of day slips softly
into its velvet cask of night,
All wrapped in folds of muslin gold
and rose pillows, shimmering bright.
Deft twilight sketches the face of night
in soft chiaroscuro light;
Watch her pictures sink toward repose
in measured, slow motion flight.
They hang like slivers of memory
on the edge of a thoughtful mind,
Like familiar paintings on gallery walls
that someone left behind.
Faint shadows tell of some now gone,
those lost you can no longer find,
Like startling gaps in a story,
or an eye gone sadly blind.
You try to decipher vague outlines…
a faded scribble, a word;
And you harken to long lost echoes
of sounds you believe you have heard.
It all feels strangely familiar;
there's a flutter stirs in your heart;
Seems sometime, somewhere along the way
you once played a crucial part!

MOUNTAIN PSALM

Silent, she sits at the edge of a stream,
Deep in reminiscence, lost in a dream;
Her lofty brow softly furrowed in thought,
On her face a distant memory caught.

Astral forests, sun-spangled gold and green,
Fit throne for this sapient and sublime queen.
The valley her footstool, the stars her crown,
Dark-wooded and snow-hooded peaks her gown.

Hear her poetry lilt in mountain rill,
Like some whisp'ring muse with a crystal quill.
Her capricious voice croons in woodland fall;
Sweet siren wrapped in a spun silver caul.

Thru wild-flow'r thicket, thru wild-berry brake
Meadows of majesty down to the lake.
Priceless sapphire in an emerald chalice,
Like some crusted jewel in a sultan's palace.

Proud peaks touch the edge of the sunset's rim,
Mellow mists roll over night's dusky brim.
She sits and she smiles, her head in her hand,
As she gazes across the slumb'ring land.

Born of the rainfall and bred by the sun,
Winnowed by winds blowing by on the run;
Sometimes untamed, sometimes halcyon and calm,
Regal Queen of Mountains, sing your sweet psalm!

THE GIFT

If it be an angel you seek, my love, you must needs look elsewhere. Alas, I would hardly measure up, for I am not nearly good enough and I sadly lack the requisite beauty. In truth, my neighbor would not find it hard to outshine me, like the moon outshines the stars. But, if perchance it is true wealth you seek – ah, then perhaps your quest is ended! And yet, ere I bare my gift before you, a word of warning. Do not set your sights on tawdry gilt. What I offer may not seem much by the rich man's standards; yet, before you scoff beloved, pause and consider – this tiny gift, innocent of ribbon or gilding, invisible to a clouded eye, no more than a ripple in the boundless ocean of time, is the greatest truth man has known; the essence of all life and creation. Like the pulsing throb of the evening star that fills the dusk with silver light, its beauty has transformed the world since time immemorial. A lucky few stumble upon it along the path of life. Others spend their lives in vain pursuit. If found, then, like an uncut diamond, it is theirs to make of it what they will. Such is the gift of love. I offer it to you. Tell me, will it suffice?

MONSOON HERALD

A breaking thunderstorm darkens
the blue face of the sky
And mars the sunlight frieze, spilt gold
thru dancing leaves.
A hush, a pause, a sudden quickening in the air,
Expectant nature holds her breath, and all is still.
Then, wild and savage horses rent the summer's day
With sudden thund'rous hooves that flash,
With cloud-misted breath of lightening-burst and clash,
And gale from tumbled, windswept mane…
All streak the trembling heavens and
lash the shuddering world.
Then lo, a calm, a waiting stillness follows;
The only muffl'd sound a gentle, dripping silence,
Soft footfalls of the departing rain that washed away
The darkness from the face of this
old, time-worn earth...

DUSKFALL

As mantled dusk begins to fall, sifting through the shifting shadows of silent evening, it lays a veiled pathway for the moonlit footsteps of approaching night; the evening star, gloaming's radiant herald, lights the first flickering lamp of the nightsky. Then, soft as thistledown, come those little sounds of nature: the hushed, whispered prayers rising from the earth, and the rustling breezes of heaven's gentle benedictions as all God's creatures fall into slumber. It is that time of day when, for a moment, the world stands poised; and in the still, the music of the hemispheres may be heard, blowing on the wind where soul meets soul. All at once, the old peepul tree drops its last autumn leaf, like a sudden exclamation in the silence! Startled, the world stirs, gathers itself, then slowly returns to its rest once more.

OBSERVATIONS

What is judged to be wrong, what is judged to be right…
With merits purchased by standards of money and might,
There's a hard and fast rule that dictates who will win –
To be rich is an honour, to be poor is a sin.

To grow in stature from year to year,
So that life may fit one like a measured glove.
To perpetuate beauty of mind and soul,
To attain heights of perception
Through an open, curious and deferential mind;
Rather than diminish in size into a relic,
So that time hangs loosely like a shrunken,
Senile garment of little use and no enhancement.

The sepia etchings in the gallery of my mind do not
fade with the passage of years.
Rich and abundant, they shine through the hallways of
time and deny effacement.

May love and kindness be the hyphens in my life,
Understanding and tolerance its commas,
Contentment and gratitude the fullstop at its end.

Would that my life were as resplendent as spring, as replete as summer, a journey that leads through an autumn of serenity toward the contentment of a peaceful winter.

Love is the champagne of life;
The world is well lost within its bubbles!

Fortune sits carding the tangled skeins of life, deaf to all supplicants who come knocking at her door, carrying their burdens, and offering their prayers, in hope of some small measure of benevolence.

OFFERINGS...

I shall pass your way but once, beloved,
And like a flower, I shall let fall my life at your feet.
There, with the imminent promise of a bud
About to blossom and unfurl its petals,
I shall await the life-giving dew of your love,
So that I may offer to you my heart, my soul, my all.
Do not hesitate long, my beloved,
Perchance you forfeit the moment
And I wither away by the roadside.

I hear your voice, beloved, like a child's in the wilderness;
I stretch forth my hand but, alas, you cannot see it for
confusion.

Uphold me, beloved, for I am nigh broken, and heavy
of heart my spirit wanders down the long and troubled
corridors of life, seeking a light in the darkness. I carry
my lamp; it is held at the ready…waiting to be lit…

Should you open your hand and set me free,
I would fold my petals like a forgotten flower,

I would droop to the ground,
I would breathe my last and die.
For what am I without you –
Like a tree without its leaves,
Like a breeze without its song,
Like an ocean without its shore,
Like a day without the sun,
Ah, like a night bereft of its moon…

DEVOTIONS

As a bewildered child would turn to a parent in trust, so
I come to you with faith and ask – what would you have
me do, where would you have me go? I am but an errant
child who turns to you in times of trouble; is there a
sheltering haven for every wandering spirit such as I?

Lord, take my hand and hold it fast;
I feel my sight has cleared at last.
Perhaps You'll let me take a seat
To sing my song here, at Your feet.
Though my words be poor, the tune off-key,
All shall improve if You bear with me.
I have not much – all I have to give
Is this small soul and the life I live…

The Hidden Storm…
Ah Lord! For what purpose was I made?
Such thoughts and passions surge and fade
To leave me spent and torn between
Shadowy glimmerings barely seen.
I struggle within myself and strain
A tenuous insight to attain
As, often times, I rebel and cry

And pour pleading questions at the sky.
But all effort falls short of gain
As I teeter 'twixt turmoil and pain.
I cannot count the wrongs I've done,
Or the empty races I have run,
Shed many a wasted sigh and tear
On the thorny path that brought me here.
If You would silence this storm that blows,
You could bring this tumult to a close;
Fend off dark shadows of care and woe,
Then, plant in their stead a peace to grow
And flow'r within this consenting breast.
Ah Lord, put this fevered mind to rest!

REMEMBRANCE*

In my soul, beloved, I can feel that you and I
Have traversed many worlds together, hand in hand;
For we are one, you and I, and like a song,
Some whispered echo on the breath of eternity,
Together, we shall traverse many more.

My thoughts of you aspire heavenward
Like the sweet-scented woodsmoke of autumn fires;
My mind is strewn with many-hued memories
That rustle like the restless, whispering leaves of fall,
Filling my soul with a remembered love.

* From: *Where Destiny Commands*
      1939–1945: A Time of Love & War

ABSENCE

How do I fill this empty space?
Who can I find to take your place?
Who told you it was time to go?
What makes you think that you could know
My strength of will to be alone,
To sit here, waiting, by the phone!
Who'll hold me safely in the night,
And be there still by morning light?
Who'll laugh and love me when I go wrong,
And be my strength when I'm not strong?
Who'll play, and tease, and cosset me,
Then help me face reality?
Who'll do the things that I can't do,
Like fix my laptop to work like new!
Or change the bulb of my bedside light
When it's fused and I'd like to read at night!
You know, this sort of thing won't do –
Simply nothing's the same without you!
Like a breakfast of eggs and toast and tea
Won't go down well when there's only me;
A stroll on the beach, a walk thru the park,
Pastimes quite useless for one to embark.
I suppose I could rant, rave, or sigh…
Or curl up small and have a good cry.
But what would I gain if I lost my head?

So, I'll take up pen and paper instead:
Hello darling, I'm fine and having fun.
Today I got loads of important stuff done.
Saw a great movie, met someone for lunch,
Got quite tiddly swilling champagne punch.
Tomorrow, no doubt, will prove hectic too;
So you see, dear, I'm doing fine without you!
How about you? I do hope you're well;
Haven't heard from you, so it's hard to tell.
Not that I worry! Life's far too sublime
With picnics and parties that take up my time.
Friends are a-plenty, they've really been grand,
Their laughter and antics always at hand.
Not a dull moment, no time to be blue,
To wonder or worry with so much to do.
But, now and then, for no reason at all,
I find myself wondering if you'll chance to call.
And sly as you please, like a thief in the night,
A memory steals through, casting a blight
Of shadows, of longing that will not let go,
A reminder you've gone and...*drat*! I *do* miss you so!

COME FLY WITH ME

Good morning!
How are you, madam? Welcome aboard.
Yes, sir, your veg meal's been catered, rest assured.
I'm the Indian stewardess, on board just for you;
The others, as you will see, are all 'foreign' crew.
I'm handpicked from hundreds of young
hopefuls, they say –
Schooled, uniformed, and prepped for this
glamorous display.
I float down the aisle in my silk sari so bright,
Yet, I manage my duties, be they heavy or light.
Without doubt we're by far the most versatile set,
Trained for Tristar, VC10 *and* Jumbo Jet.
Beg pardon? Oh dear! A moment if you please, sir,
I shall try to find someone to translate for her.
You see, I'm from Bengal, I can manage Hindi too.
My prowess, sadly, does not include Telegu.
Store hand luggage and coats in your overhead bin.
Sir, cussing and swearing won't help your bag fit in!
A carrycot for your child? Indeed, we have six.
Yes, a seventh babe would find itself in a fix.
But infant food and nappies are no problem at all,
When you need those amenities, just give me a call.
A portable potty for your wee one to use?
If I had one, dear madam, I would not refuse!

What! You have brought your own stove to cook your
own food??
I insist you desist, sir! Not at this altitude!
Whiskey soda? Bloody Mary? Tonic and gin?
For me? On duty? Good sir, don't tempt me to sin!
Apologies, sir, but all the loos are engaged.
Stop! You can't use the ice bucket!!! Too late I'm afraid…
Forgive me, sir, it appears we're all out of coke.
No indeed, sir, that was definitely no joke.
And we can't use the ice. Why? I suggest you don't ask!
Chucked it, bucket and all. A most unpleasant task!
Now we've run out of sodas and tonics as well.
The next six hours, without doubt, are sure to be hell!
Ah, here comes our good Captain to see how we fare.
Don't panic sir! The plane's safe in our copilot's care.
Stewardess, where are we now, and what's that down there?
Madam – that is terra firma, and we're up in the air.
Steward, what time is it? Might be time for my pill.
Sir, up here in the clouds, we find all time stands still.
Nonstop call bells to answer, not a moment's respite;
Umpteen meals, hot and cold, have been served through
the flight.
Finally! The announcement for landing goes out,
Fasten seat belts, stow tables; please, no walking about.
The lone six-year-old in our care*, we've brought him
home safe,
Now we'll hand him to ground staff, the poor little waif!
Our landing gear's down. Hurrah! We are
now on the ground,

A rush for the exits; farewells exchanged all round.
One more flight to our credit, thank heavens it's done
Sans much drama or bloodshed – a fairly smooth run.
Hotel room at last! A well-earned rest and some play.
Shelve all thought of the next flight –
We made it today!!!

* Small child unaccompanied by an adult guardian, travelling in the care of cabin crew.

CITY BY THE BAY

Far and forlorn comes the ghostly call
Of a foghorn, warning seafarers all:
The ocean is deep, and the night is dark,
The reefs are treacherous, sharp and stark.
The sentinel bridge stands guard at the gate
Of the haven known as the Golden State.

Past infamous island hunched in the bay,
Keeper of secrets from back in the day
When sinners and sirens came looking for gold,
In hopes of amassing great fortunes untold.
The city lies stilled, now, in fitfull sleep,
Stirred only by dreams history left in her keep.

The fog, like a cat, prowls hill and hollow;
A full moon keeps watch as shadows follow,
Around a corner and up a dark street,
Wraith-like they tiptoe on phantom feet.
But look, to the east! Light grows in the sky!
The night with its moon and shadows must fly.

The city awakens, life starts to flow,
She is hustle and bustle, all on the go.
Cable-cars climb streets with breathtaking views,

Painted Ladies* arrayed in glorious hues.
Be she shrouded in mist, or kissed by the sun –
She is feted in song for the hearts she has won!

* Decorated Victorian houses of San Francisco, famously known as Painted Ladies

MY CAT

My companion, the Cat.
Not thin. Not fat.
Marshmallow paws
Hide manicured claws.
Pert, pointed ears,
Pink tongue that peers
Through tiny, pearly-white teeth.
And just beneath
Complacent grin,
Smug velvet chin;
On top, a soot-smudgeoned nose.
A wiggle that grows
At the other end.
My beguiling friend
With the golden eyes
That can tell such lies!
Chic, elegant fur,
A dulcet purr,
Curled tight in a ball
Or languorous sprawl,
Such an innocent face
I have seen no place.
On no other cat.
Not thin. Not fat.

FATHER

Father! My Father! Light of my life!
Beacon that held at bay heartache and strife.
With pure, boundless love you sheltered me,
As you nurtured the years of my infancy!
I often recall looking way up high,
With a wide-eyed child's adoring sigh –
My Father, he is so tall and strong,
Did growing up take him very long?
Could he once have been as small as me
Held safe, like this, on his father's knee?
With infinite care you helped me grow,
Your love my shield against storms that blow
Through teenage years, till you made me stand;
Then, gentle and wise, you withdrew your hand.
Through life's many toils, from start to end,
You remained my beloved, most steadfast friend.
Heart of my heart, part of my soul,
You shared yours with me, making mine whole.
You blest me with life, your strength built my will,
Your blessings and strength uphold me still.
Your dear face, a memory caught in my heart;
Your smile bids 'Take courage, no matter life's path'.
Yes, though you are gone, I feel you, still here,
Standing beside me, Father most dear.

MOTHER

Ah, Mother mine, so tender and wise,
Who gave me abode, love-light in your eyes.
My cradle your womb, your heart bound to mine,
Your nurt'ring body your daughter's lifeline.
No matter how far, no matter how near,
Through joy and laughter or sorrowing tear,
A bond such as this may never be broken,
Of such a love no word can be spoken.
Your blessings remain, though you are gone.
Your strenghth guides me, Mother, your love-light
shines on.

ACKNOWLEDGEMENTS

My deep gratitude and thanks to Sriharsha Nagaraj, my dear friend who was instrumental in bringing this little body of work out from the shadows and into the light. My special thanks to the many friends, past and present, who inspired and encouraged me when I needed it the most. And last, but not least, my thanks to Sarvatmika Rajeev of Notion Press for her patience in bringing it all together, and to all those in the wings who did their part in helping to ready this book for its readers.

www.ingramcontent.com/pod-product-compliance
Lightning Source LLC
Chambersburg PA
CBHW052221150726
48002CB00003B/1223